YOUR CHILD
HAVE A
GREAT DAY AT
SCHOOL

BY ROBIN McCLURE

SOURCEBOOKS, INC.®
NAPERVILLE, ILLINOIS

Published by Sourcebooks, Inc.
P.O. Box 4410, Naperville, Illinois 60567-4410
(630) 961-3900
Fax: (630) 961-2168
www.sourcebooks.com

Printed and bound in the United States of America.
VP 10 9 8 7 6 5 4 3 2 1

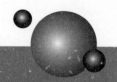

Acknowledgments

Just as most people would agree that it is not easy being a parent, the same can certainly be said about being a teacher. Each school year, teachers are assigned a classroom full of unique students at different stages and abilities, who they essentially "raise," from an academic and social standpoint, only to have to say good-bye at year-end. The cycle then begins anew come fall.

As a parent of three children (two are in elementary school), my admiration of teachers continues to grow along with my kids every academic year. I get the privilege of getting to know my childrens' teachers, coaches, assistants, and support staff throughout the year, in part through one-on-one conferences, but also by volunteering and sometimes simply observing from afar. Of course, I also get to relive many magical classroom moments (and some not so much) through the enthusiastic retelling of stories and experiences my youngsters share at the end of each day. It is almost mind-boggling how regardless of the weather, the way they feel, or how the class interacts, teachers enter their classrooms with a smile and come prepared to teach and for kids to learn. They do this day after day, year after year, and most profess they couldn't imagine doing anything else!

The ideas shared in this book have largely come from dedicated early educators but also from parents who love them. I am privileged to have classroom teachers in my own life, starting with my own mother, Bonnie Watkins; my sister-in-law, Susan Watkins; and my niece, Jessica Owen. But my "family" of teachers extends far beyond them. In particular, I would like to dedicate this book to the Birdville Independent School District (BISD) and the Grapevine-Colleyville Independent School District (GCISD), both located in northeast Tarrant County, Texas, with whom I worked in an administrative role for thirteen-plus years. In particular, I offer my absolute adoration of the caring and involved staff members at BISD's W. A. Porter Elementary, who truly embrace *every* child and give each student the power of knowledge through learning. A great majority of ideas are from the hearts and minds of the dedicated team members there, and without them, the idea for this book would not have been born.

Introduction

Except for the fast-paced and seemingly miraculous changes that occur in the first year of life, the elementary school years are perhaps the greatest time of change and growth in a young child. First grade is a huge transition from preschool and kindergarten, where the focus from learning through play shifts to reading and writing. Each progressive year incurs additional subjects, more homework, and greater expectations. Seat time (when kids sit in their chairs for extended periods of learning) increases, and a child's interest in friendships, extracurricular activities, and fitting in socially expands. Kids who begged parents to eat lunch with them only last month may suddenly prefer that Mom and Dad stay home so they can sit next to their friends.

Along with this growing independence and maturity comes the pressure of responsibility, the development of good (or not so good) study habits, and peer pressure. And through all these changes, from the first year of a child's elementary school experience to the final days before secondary school, teachers agree that it is parents who have the ability to make the greatest difference. Parents committed to and supportive of their child's education and school success can make a significant impact on whether a child's school experience is one of excitement…or of dread.

Helping your child to have a positive attitude about school is something that often takes work and effort to achieve. While some children just naturally seem to love school and bounce out of their homes eager to begin the day, most kids have to be coaxed out of their warm beds in the morning. They struggle with the structured routine and having to do homework after a long day of school. The way you approach these routines and requirements can stay with your child long after the elementary school years are but a memory.

So, how do you get your child started on the road to a positive mental attitude at school? Well, there's a lot more to helping your child feel good about school than getting enough sleep and eating a nutritional breakfast! And that's where this book comes in.

151 Ways to Help Your Child Have a Great Day at School is filled with tried-and-true advice from early childhood classroom teachers who each day experience what works—and what doesn't—when it comes to parent support, homework, and evening and morning routines. Helpful tips and motivational suggestions are also provided by parents-in-the-know, child-care workers, and even kids themselves to help your child start the day off with a smile and a positive attitude—each and every day, all year long!

1. **Use everyday life to show the connections between school subjects and real-world experience.**

   Elementary-aged kids don't necessarily understand *why* they are learning all the things they are in school and can quickly assume that certain subjects are a waste of time when it comes to real life. Help your children to see the connection between academic subjects, such as language arts, science, grammar, history, and art, and everyday situations. For example, having your child read street signs will help her understand that all stop signs are the same shape and color and use the same letters, which in turn helps her understand how the world connects.

2. **Incorporate subject-themed family nights into your life, making them fun and positive**

learning experiences at the same time.

Kids may not "get" that cooking involves sequencing (the order in which you do it), math (how do you get ¾ cup of sugar when you only have a ½ and ¼ measuring cup?), and science (how do you melt hard butter, or why does gelatin get thick?). Make one night a week a different subject, and let your elementary-age child pick the subject. Suggest a couple of options that fit into that night's subject. Soon, your child will literally be begging for math night (cutting a pizza into a certain number of pieces and then serving them equally to all family members counts) and other subject nights, much to the astonishment of friends and the delight of your child's teacher!

3. Incorporate learning into vacations and other special times to foster a love of lifelong learning.

Kids can learn outside the classroom setting, so take time away from structured learning and go on adventures to explore your child's passions or imagination. If your child is fascinated with pirates, for example, visit a marina and look at different types of boats, or have a treasure hunt at the beach. These are great ways to fuel your child's future interests and enhance her knowledge at the same time. If you vacation in the mountains, look for rocks that show various striations, or explain to your child how a mountain is formed. Traveling through a historic town can invite discussions about history, such as why houses were built the way they were or what industry caused the town to form.

4. **Don't just encourage your child to read; model the behavior by reading yourself.**

How many parents just tell their kids to go into their room and complete their reading assignment? Children learn by modeling, so adults in the house need to read too (without the television on). Have a quick discussion at dinner or in the car about topics you've each read about that day. Parents should ask kids about their reading, but children should have quality opportunities to ask adults questions, too! By third or fourth grade, kids can begin reading the newspaper and may find enjoyment in certain sections that are of special interest to them (like sports, life, family, or current events). Consider turning newspaper reading into a family routine (being sure to shelter children from any inappropriate news that may be reported). Establishing a routine of keeping up with current events from the newspaper will not only help your child to be a better reader, but a more-informed citizen as well. Start young kids looking at the daily weather graphs and cartoons (you can read strips to emerging readers). Clip out articles for your young child to read and then discuss with you. Being able to learn about current worldwide events on a timely basis will also foster curiosity and greater international interest.

5. **Develop a truly positive and memorable parent/teacher relationship.**

Sadly, teachers report that while this may seem the simplest of ways to achieve success in school, a positive parent/teacher relationship is the exception, rather than the rule, with many families. Parents may attend meet-the-teacher nights or school functions, and may even participate in an annual parent/teacher conference and class party, but that is still a superficial relationship. To really establish a strong relationship and truly understand how your child learns and acts at school, foster ongoing ways to keep in touch with your child's teacher. Find out the teacher's preferred way to communicate (note that it may not be yours), and then do so regularly. Whether it is writing notes, phone calls, email, or formal conferences, think of it as a yearlong partnership. Using the teacher's preferred way to communicate (remember, there are many more kids than just yours in the classroom) encourages open communication about your child's strengths, challenges, issues, and concerns throughout the school year.

6. Pay as much attention to your child's conduct grades as subject grades.

Of course, grades are important. With today's emphasis on academic rigor, kids feel the pressure of performing well each and every day. However, parents should instill in their kids the understanding that how they act at school—toward their fellow classmates as well as their teachers—is just as important as their academic performance. Conduct grades provide insight into how a child is performing at school, the way she interacts with others, and whether she listens well and follows instructions. If a poor conduct grade is due to more serious reasons than talking, not listening, or following directions (i.e., hitting someone or saying inappropriate things), then don't hesitate to take corrective action. You don't want a bad conduct grade to become a regular occurrence.

7. Don't let your morning stress and bad moods ruin the day for your kids.

Let's face it. Most of us are pretty cranky in the mornings, and who can help but feel stressed when everyone in the family is rushing around trying to eat breakfast, get dressed, brush hair and teeth, make sure all work is completed and put in the right place in the backpack, and then on their way…on time…every weekday! However, mornings are truly the mood maker or breaker of the day, and teachers report that a kid who starts the day sad or mad rarely overcomes the mood to have a successful school day. Do everything in your power to make every morning go smoothly. Save any discipline discussions, grumbles, and, in general, *anything* that could be a downer to a child for after school. A child's send-off to school each morning should include a hug, a positive affirmation of support, enthusiasm over the lessons planned for the day, any schedule reminders, and an "I love you" from you!

8. **Encourage classroom friendships by arranging playdates outside of the school day with kids who are good personality matches with your child.**

Some kids are instant social butterflies and make a classroom of "best friends" in the first week of each school year. Others may be more reserved and take longer to develop friends. Ask your child's teacher whom your child seems to match up with in the classroom, and take the initiative to invite that child over for a playdate. Kids who have friends who they look forward to seeing at school each day tend to have a more positive school experience.

9. **Remember that it takes a village to raise a child, so don't hesitate to call in support as needed to ensure your child is succeeding in school.**

While the elementary years may seem to be an awfully early time to start worrying about a child's success in school, the truth is that being in tune with your child from kindergarten on up can help stop small problems or challenges from turning into bigger ones. While you should always start with your child's teacher first, there is no reason parents can't also initiate meetings with the school administrator, counselor, and even resource assistants to discuss concerns, approaches, or other ways to ensure your child is having the best experience possible. A good teacher won't be offended if you reach out past her classroom; often, a counselor or administrator can offer additional ideas on certain topics, such as making and keeping friends (or staying away from bad influences) that may not be appropriate for a classroom teacher to suggest.

10. **Don't let your child see your disappointment in a bad grade. Instead, use the grade as a sign that you need to step up your homework support at home.**

Kids, even those as young as kindergarten age, can fixate on grades, and your response to their grades can determine how they feel about their intelligence, self-worth, and even your love for them. While everyone wants their child to score 100s and As on every report card, logic prevails that it won't always happen (and remember that a C is still considered average). As the elementary learning years progress, it becomes harder and harder for a child to maintain a straight-A average. Praise your child for outstanding work, while using lower grades as an opportunity to have one-on-one academic time in a positive setting. Try using comments like, "Tonight after dinner, let's look at the story together," or, "I can't wait to see how well you're doing with your math facts. Let's practice with those flash cards over dessert!"

11. **Don't over-praise your child's efforts. Instead, try and temper the "attaboys" for efforts truly earned so youngsters will continuously strive for best effort.**

Many child experts have cautioned that it's easy for parents to go overboard in their zeal to foster a child's self-esteem. As a result, there are a lot of young children with a false sense of their abilities, who think they are truly marvelous in every aspect of their lives. Often, this means the work ethic and effort may not be as strong as you'd like in later years. If your child has truly created an artistic, age-appropriate masterpiece, then say so. But if he's simply scribbled a few objects haphazardly onto a page and shows it off, you're not doing him any real service by oohing and aahing over it. Instead, comment on a special shape or color choice, but don't rush to put it on the refrigerator or call Grandma. Save those moments (and there will be many) for work or effort that should truly make him proud!

12. Don't correct your child's homework or help out with

the answers. Your job is to coach and assist, but not to "do."

While it may seem harmless to add a letter to a misspelled word or erase extreme messiness from a project that is to be turned in, you're really only doing your child a disservice in the end. After all, which provides the better learning moment: Your child getting a 100 on a project that you've done a "tiny bit" of corrections on, or a 75 due to misspellings and sloppiness? Teachers report that they can always spot a parent assist on projects. In other words, if a child who struggles with spelling in the classroom or doesn't color within the lines or cut cleanly during classroom projects turns in a perfectly produced project from home, isn't it obvious that there was help?

13. Know that kids talk about absolutely everything that happens at home while at school.

If you tell your child not to talk about something that happened at home, you can almost be assured that the action or event will be openly discussed in the classroom, at least among friends, the next day. If you don't want your child repeating that she saw Daddy in his underwear or that you called an upcoming required classroom project "an absolutely stupid thing to require of third graders," then, well, you know what you shouldn't do! Kids talk, and school is an outlet for them to speak their minds. Luckily, most teachers are well-trained in redirecting conversations in which too much information seems to be flowing.

14. If a life change is occurring at home and affecting your child, consider alerting his teacher.

Sensitive issues like divorce, a major illness, and other private family matters that you'd like to stay private, most likely won't. You can help by readily providing information that could affect your child's focus (such as a grandparent's death, any change in family status, or even a new baby) to your child's teacher, to help her be equipped for any emotional changes. School personnel may be restricted to ask you about specific family details, but you can provide as much information you feel appropriate to help a child through any life transition period. A good teacher will also be in tune enough with a child's emotions to know when to call a parent or the school counselor to help a struggling child cope.

15. Regularly talk to your child about your own challenges in school and what you did to overcome them.

Be honest about any challenges or struggles you had in school, and describe what your solutions were. Give specific examples, such as, "I really had a hard time with reading when I started first grade and went to tutorials for three years until I felt comfortable with my skills." However, don't doom a child to the same academic fate as you may have felt you had by saying to others, "She's having a hard time in math—she gets that from me." Point out your strengths, and theirs as well.

16. Each day after school, ask your child what were the three BEST things that happened at school.

Make this question a daily ritual,

but keep it fun and positive. There's only one rule: The three best things cannot be repeated from any previous day's "best" list for that week. After your child has named the three things, ask questions and discuss them. You can even have every family member (Mom and Dad included) list their three BESTS over dinner each evening to encourage additional conversation!

17. Resist the urge to become a school gossip.

No one likes to gossip…at least that's what everyone says. However, it's easy to start second-guessing administrative decisions, a prohibition made by your child's teacher, or the selection of an "undeserving" child for an award. Well-meaning parents may begin discussing these opinions, and before they know it, there is an unintentional mutiny on their hands.

Invariably, a parent will make comments in front of a child who then repeats it, and so on. If you have a concern, address it directly with a teacher or campus staff member, and then be supportive of any decisions that are made. Know that you may not have the full story or the background necessary to totally understand and consider the interests of all children.

18. Praise publicly and criticize privately.

Your child may not necessarily like or agree with the teacher or the school's rules, and may even exaggerate or offer his perspective on events to get you to take a side. But parents should never get caught up in a teacher-child-parent tug-of-war. If your child talks about something that happened in school that was "not fair" or says that the teacher was "picking on him," be careful to not overreact or to tell your child you're going to fix the problem. Instead, listen carefully to your child's perspective, and then repeat back to him exactly what he said occurred. Let your child know that you want to get all the facts straight first, and that you want to be very sure that you have a total understanding (also allowing for any corrections to statements your child has made). Then, without rendering judgment or expressing an opinion (that you may regret having said later), simply indicate that you will speak with the teacher. And then do exactly that. You may find that your child lost a privilege, for example, because of something he did or didn't do in accordance with classroom rules or school policy. There could also be a misunderstanding that you can help to clear up. But unless the situation is indeed a true concern, parents and teachers should agree and be on the same side, and the child should clearly see that they work together. That way, a child cannot play one adult against another for a perceived benefit.

19. Volunteer your time in the classroom.

Teachers typically welcome extra helping hands in the classroom. And what better way to truly understand your child's school schedule and academic and social expectations than to view firsthand what happens during the school day? As academic rigor continues to increase and necessary skills are taught at increasingly early ages (most kindergartners receive time in a computer lab, for example), one set of hands is simply not enough. Carve out some time, volunteer whatever amount you can give, and always deliver as promised.

Just remember that regardless of your position outside the classroom, in the classroom you are volunteering as a caring parent who will gladly pitch in and help wherever needed.

20. Don't do the helicopter hover.

Don't become a "hovering helicopter" parent at school. Studies show that parents who hover over their kids, constantly "doing" things for them and offering never-ending support, are actually raising kids who aren't able to cope with college and life on their own. If you volunteer at your child's school, remember that you are there as an adult volunteer for *all* children and should equally help every child—not just yours—with the task at hand. If you're just volunteering so you can see whom your child sits next to or because you think your child will be proud of your presence, recheck your priorities.

Your motivation and focus should be completely on the kids, and not on yourself.

21. Confidentiality is essential in the classroom.

Most schools beg for helping hands, but a quick deal-breaker is repeating confidential information. Privacy laws are designed to keep a child's health and personal information private, and schools have plans in place to keep that information confidential. Parents who regularly volunteer at a campus may witness children receiving tutorial assistance, being pulled out for resources or special education assistance, or even receiving counseling support. All such information is private. You are expected to attend to your tasks and not make comments about any observations you've witnessed, or else you could be in violation of these privacy

protections. Even desperately needed volunteers won't be asked back
if loose lips or nosy actions compro-
mise a child's placement at school.
If you are in doubt as to what you
can talk about, check with your
child's teacher.

22. Check your ego at the door when entering your child's school or classroom.

You might be a security expert, a
computer whiz, or owner of a public
relations firm. But when you enter
your child's school, your role is as a
parent or as a volunteer. If you have
talents to share, then by all means
offer them in the process established
at the campus or district level. While
most volunteer offers are gladly
accepted, a person who laments
that the school's computer software
is inadequate or that the decora-
tions made for a school play are too

amateurish isn't going to find the welcome mat extended for long. Parents need to check their egos at the front door and approach a child's school with respect. Being a CEO of a large company is indeed impressive; however, what you do for a living or how much you volunteer should not in any way influence classroom favors or special access to your child's teacher.

23. Resist the urge to compare.

It's easy to fall in the trap of comparing your child's accomplishments and skills to those of another—but don't. Educators agree that every child learns at a different pace, and certain things will always come more easily or more difficult to some kids than others. Just because your child reads independently when entering kindergarten, for example, doesn't mean that she will be any more academically advanced than her peer group in the fourth grade. Be on the lookout for your child making comparisons, as well, and put a stop to it at once. Depending on where your child falls in the comparison game, she may suffer from low self-esteem or develop an inflated view of herself, neither of which is a trait you want her to carry through school.

24. Set a goal for helping out throughout your child's entire school career.

Most kindergarten teachers report that there are often more volunteers than there is work that needs to be done. That's because parents are eager to see their youngsters begin school on a positive note, and volunteering is a way to help see their child during the day and ensure he is adjusting to school. By fifth or sixth grade, however, teachers are scrambling to find any helping hands. While early education activities may be more "fun" for volunteers, assistance is arguably even more greatly needed in higher grades, where activities and projects are more difficult, and tutoring is also urgently needed. The need for volunteers continues to intensify at the middle school levels as well. Parents should set a realistic schedule for what they can do to help their child's school and then carry out that goal throughout the school years. You won't regret the extra time spent—guaranteed!

25. Frequently check and restock your child's school supplies.

You've purchased the full array of school supplies for the school year, so your child should be all set… right? Most likely not. Kids devour school supplies at an astonishing pace. Some kids love to sharpen pencils—so much so that a nub can be all that remains after a few days. That box of tissues that started the year won't last long for a child with allergies. Some kids either forget to tell their parents or are embarrassed to let their teacher know that they're out of something, and school supplies should never stress or hinder a child. So don't wait until your teacher or child says something to you. Rather, restock regularly or ask what is running low.

26. Don't pack lunches that are hard to open, require preparation, or are unappetizing.

Elementary kids sometimes have trouble opening the "convenience" packaging that tempts parents for quick and easy meals. Soft-pouch drinks with an attached straw, for example, can be difficult to open and insert for younger hands. Vacuum-sealed items are often ripped open by young kids, sometimes with the contents ending up all over the floor. Because kids often don't want to ask for help (or because there are relatively few adults monitoring lunch for a great number of children), the food you packed may not get eaten. Keep in mind that kids will throw away unappetizing food, even if it's nutritionally sound. (Bruised banana, anyone?) The result is a hungry, grumpy child who may not be able to effectively focus on the afternoon's lessons.

27. Don't raise a "star"—raise a team player.

School plays, musicals, and special activities and events are often big parts of an elementary child's school year. Learning lines, singing new songs, or participating in the science fair, spelling bee, or "Battle of the Books" competitions foster life skills of studying, memorization, teamwork, and motivation. While every child is a star waiting to shine, keep check of your expectations for your youngster. Encourage, but don't push your child into an activity, and equally praise the child who is a stage hand and the one who gets to sing a solo.

28. Encourage independence in your child.

Now that your child is in school, it's time to start letting go...a concept that's difficult for any parent. Keep in mind that a child who is able to increasingly make his or her own decisions (and face the consequences that go with them) will make for a stronger, more successful student in years to come. Minimize potential for battles about what to wear, when to do homework, and even what type of backpack to carry by empowering your child to make simple decisions.

29. Teach planning and organization techniques early and ongoing.

A key way to foster school readiness and success is to teach your child planning techniques now...even in first grade! Your child's school may or may not use a daily planner, but regardless, you can create a planner at home. Consider buying a weekly or monthly dry-erase style that can be hung at a level that your child can view and update. Younger kids can use symbols, such as stars, to show what day the weekly spelling test is, for example. Older elementary-age kids can start writing in key dates themselves, such as a spelling bee, class party, or field trip. This sets kids up to be more accountable for their own work and to learn the importance of preparation and meeting deadlines.

30. Cue in to any signs about how your child is fitting in.

Whether it is a true problem or a concern that your child is harboring because of insecurity, a youngster who feels picked on or excluded by her peers is simply not going to have a great experience at school. Listen carefully to your child's concerns and don't hesitate to talk with the teacher and partner with her to help put an end to whatever is causing the problem. Do keep an open mind and consider that kids may not really be rejecting your child—perhaps they simply don't want to play the same things at recess. Or maybe they are ridiculing her "babyish" backpack. Suggest different games to play or encourage your child to consider her peers' suggestions. And if your child still likes her Elmo backpack, give her some comeback lines for any teasing. If she's not too attached to the backpack, maybe it's time to find a new older-kid option that will stop the teasing.

31. Protect your child as much as possible from the big, bad bullies.

Schools everywhere embrace the "zero tolerance" approach for certain behaviors that can harm a child physically, socially, or emotionally. If your child is being bullied, or even "feels" like he is, waste no time in stepping in and seeking an immediate remedy. That doesn't mean charging in like a bull, however. How parents respond to bullying can either help eliminate the problem or make it worse, especially for an older child. Don't hesitate to meet with the teacher to get a broader perspective of the concerns and ask what is being done to mitigate the problem. Your child should feel safe and confident that you will provide whatever support is necessary if he feels like he is being bullied. Try giving your child ideas about what to do and good comebacks for bullies' lines of attack to see if he can handle it himself. Teachers also should send a clear message to all kids in the classroom that bullying will not be tolerated and significant consequences will be rendered.

32. Recognize your child's own unlikable traits, and work together to improve behaviors.

Nobody is perfect, and as much as you love your child, recognize that she most likely has at least one trait, if not more, that isn't very likable to others. Whether it is a tendency to brag, an extreme competitive streak, or a gross habit like picking her nose, work with your child to overcome this behavior.

33. Practice the art of good sportsmanship.

Talk to your child often about the importance of not always being first, and show him how to act if he or his team finishes with disappointing results. Many kids are competitive, but you can preempt any ugly behaviors by finding out what sports your child may be learning and then working with him on the side to understand the concept of "team." He'll learn how to win *and* lose gracefully, whether it's a game or math drill.

34. Save the designer duds for special occasions.

Your child may feel like a fashion diva or class hottie in an expensive new outfit, but the day could be destroyed if paint gets spilled on the shirt or the knee gets ripped during recess. Why risk your anger and your child's anguish over the loss of a special outfit when you can avoid it all by only dressing your child in practical play clothes for school? Your child's teacher will thank you!

35. Don't let your child attend school in flip-flops, anything with heels, or hard-to-lace shoes.

Don't send your child to school in lace-up sneakers if she can't properly tie her shoes or if it takes her a very long time to accomplish the task. Choose a slip-on type instead. By the same token, leave flip-flops, heeled boots, or trendy shoes (even trendy clogs) at home. A child's shoes need to be appropriate for P.E. and recess. A teacher doesn't have time to tie everyone's shoes or help young students change out of one pair into another in time for recess. The exception is when the school has something like a "flip-flop Fridays" celebration day, and even then, kids will be required to bring sneakers for P.E.

36. To help boost self-esteem, practice game basics or P.E. skills at home.

Physical education coaches teach kids new skills and games every week to find exciting and fun ways to stay active. If your child isn't exactly athletic, don't let a lack of skills or game understanding turn what should be an energetic part of the day to dread. Help your child understand the rules (i.e., this is how you dribble a basketball) and feel more confident about play ability by practicing at home. Besides, you'll find it's fun for both of you!

37. Make sure your child knows proper table manners.

When your child starts school, lunch becomes one of the few social times when kids can relax, talk, and share a few laughs. But if your child doesn't know how to eat with age-appropriate table manners, lunch can become a time of anxiety rather than fun. Your child should know how to properly use a fork, spoon, knife, and napkin; drink without slurping; and avoid burping. (Burping contests will quickly land your little cherub at an isolation table or having lunch with the principal.) Don't think you can just go over lunchroom rules once and then call it a day. Help your child by modeling proper table manners during family dinners at home and practicing "dos and don'ts" or "what should you do if…" situations with your child. In addition, frequently remind your child about proper etiquette, including tucking the chair into the table after getting up and clearing all the dishes when through. The lunchroom monitor will love you and your child for this—guaranteed!

38. Lose the excuses.

Ask any teacher: Kids can get pretty creative in the excuses department when a project isn't done or homework is late. Teach your child that you are a "no-excuse" parent. If your child was given an assignment and didn't write it in the planner because "Sarah was kicking her underneath the desk, and she couldn't hear what was said," don't buy it. If your child comes home with an "incomplete," you need to be willing to apply an appropriate consequence and not become a softie over your child's clever reason. If you do this the first time, the child will become more creative the next. If you are ever truly in doubt, don't hesitate to ask the child's teacher directly, and let your child know your intent. Say something like this: "Michael, I want to repeat back what you told me happened to your homework assignment. Is this the way you understand it, because I am going to ask your teacher about this and want to be sure that I heard what you told me?" If there is indeed a valid reason, your child will most likely support that conversation. If not, your child may backtrack on the "dog-ate-the-homework" story.

39. Label absolutely everything!

Have you ever really looked at the piles of clothing and items that become part of a school's lost-and-found treasure trove? Every day, kids leave expensive new jackets on the playground or bus, only to forget exactly where they took it off when questioned by Mom or Dad that night. Teachers and school-bus drivers have many responsibilities, none of which includes keeping up with your child's coat, backpack, planner, or eyeglasses. If every item is labeled with your child's name, current grade, and teacher's name, however, chances are the item and your child will become quickly reunited. Don't leave anything to chance: Label supplies, shoes, and any clothing, such as coats, hats, and gloves, that could be removed due to changes in temperature.

40. Say no to jewelry at school.

Unless it is simple ear-studs, discourage your child from wearing jewelry of any kind to school. Why? Teachers indicate that kids tend to play with necklaces or clang their desks with charm bracelets, and as a result, focus less on the lessons at hand. In addition, let's face it, kid jewelry tends to be cheap and easily broken, and someone tugging on a necklace or breaking the chain accidentally (or not) can ruin a child's day.

41. Help your child learn her own process for solving problems.

If your child has a problem at school, whether it is academic or social, don't just state what you think the solution should be. Instead, work with your child to help her learn the process by considering various options and consequences and going through them to reach a solution on her own. If you supply the "right answer" (according to you, anyway), you're not teaching your child how to problem solve. Essentially, you are teaching her that she is not able to reach solutions on her own. Of course, depending on the child's age, you might share ideas or raise questions to help her get started, and if she gets frustrated, don't hesitate to step in.

42. Limit your questions, especially right after school.

In a well-meaning effort to connect with their kids, parents sometimes blast them with question after question right after school. While parents are simply trying to make conversation, children sometimes feel under attack or defensive. Kids like to decompress from a long day just like you do and are usually more than willing to answer your questions later.

43. Kids who find school difficult may not want to talk about it with you.

Some kids sail through elementary school with As on almost every project and assignment. Others make more mistakes and struggle to learn new concepts. Making mistakes and then correcting them is how kids learn—but your child may not want you to know that she is not perfect. It's easier to tell a parent that you got an A on the solar-system project, for example, than a C because not every planet was labeled properly. Emphasize to your child that nobody is perfect, and that as long as he gives his best effort, you are still proud of him. Encourage your child to talk about how he felt about the grade and what he thinks he could do next time to make it better.

44. Don't turn a road bump into a mountain.

What parent hasn't overreacted to a poor grade or note home from the teacher about attitude or behaving inappropriately? Of course you're upset, disappointed, and maybe even embarrassed over your child's actions at school on occasion. But keep in mind the "big picture" of your child's school career. Let the bump be a life lesson and don't turn it into an insurmountable boulder for your child. After all, here's betting you weren't perfect at school every day yourself!

45. Don't let homework become a battleground.

It's easy to become overly emotional about your child's homework and grades. We're parents, after all... right? But, ironically, one of the quickest ways to have a child lose excitement and enthusiasm toward school and school work is by fighting with your child all the time about it. If you find yourself becoming emotional about your child's homework, give yourself a time-out and re-approach your child when you have control of your emotions and words. You should be serving as a positive influence on homework, and a berating parent is not the example you want to set.

46. Parents should always present a unified front when it comes to their child's school, teacher, and homework assignments.

Even if you don't agree with your teacher's approach to learning or discipline, or your child keeps coming home with tales of difficult assignments or "impossible" tasks (such as learning the entire multiplication table), support the teacher in front of your child. While you can say, "That is going to be a big challenge, and I'll be glad to help you practice," you won't be doing your child any favors by taking sides. Rather, your job as a parent is to instill in your child that you will support her teacher this school year. It is not your child's place (or yours) to determine what the age-appropriate learning is for the grade, and while some assignments and expectations may seem very high, kids will rise to meet them in the end. If you have a personal concern about a grade or feel an assignment is too hard or time-consuming, then by all means talk to the teacher privately.

47. Find a tutor—quickly—if your child is consistently struggling in school.

If your child is struggling with daily homework, is not grasping concepts, and seems to be developing low self-esteem or saying he's "not smart," seek intervention at once. Some schools may offer special before- or after-school tutoring programs; others may have an aide who can assist your child or provide you with additional worksheets to help your child at home. Every kid learns at a different level and pace, so while your child may be among the last to learn one concept, he may be among the first to understand another. Teachers understand this, but they also recognize that children are easily discouraged, and will be glad to offer ways to help your child feel good about new skills being taught.

48. Be sure your child is "combed and clean" when arriving to school.

Bad breath, dirty clothes and skin, unwashed/uncombed hair, and earwax oozing out of ears are sure confidence killers. Kids *do* notice these things, as early as kindergarten, and comments can be unkind. School nurses face all sorts of "ick" factors when attending to a sick child, and often note that hygiene is greatly lacking, teeth appear uncared for, and that clothes and skin are dirty—

even among kids who come from middle-class households.

49. Your child probably needs deodorant and undergarments by late elementary school, even if you don't think she does.

By fourth or fifth grade, your child most likely will begin to perspire and develop body odor. Don't believe it? Just go into an older elementary child's classroom after a day of school and "smell" for yourself. Better yet, ask a teacher. Of course, perspiration is normal and is another sign kids are growing up. The same notion applies with girls and undergarments. Thin shirts that are perfectly acceptable on younger girls may not be appropriate for budding pre-teens. To maintain healthy self-esteem and prevent any teasing or unwanted attention, be sure you keep track of your child's maturity, and add undergarments as soon as you see a sign it is time.

50. Arm your child with a personal-size hand sanitizer, and replace it frequently.

Superbugs, such as drug-resistant strains of staph infections, have been in the news recently, and there is simply no downside to giving your child an extra personal health protection in addition to hand-washing routines. Teachers will be supportive of your child keeping hand sanitizer at her desk to help protect against common childhood ailments—a teacher doesn't want her classroom any more "germy" than you do!

51. Don't send your child to school sick...please!

Isn't it ironic how a parent will grumble over seeing a sneezing, hacking child in her own child's classroom, but be quick to explain away her own child's symptoms of sickness? Classrooms are a harbor for germs, and when kids are kept indoors and in close quarters during inclement weather periods, the risk of spreading illnesses becomes greater. Your school has written policies on when to keep kids at home. Most require a child to remain fever-free for forty-eight hours before returning to school, or to have a doctor's note before being readmitted after having contagious illnesses, such as strep throat, flu, pinkeye, and a host of others. Teachers and school nurses talk about how the "plague" can reduce a classroom of twenty healthy kids to twelve or thirteen in just days. Your child may not earn a perfect attendance trophy this year if you keep her at home when ill, but the teacher and your child's friends will give you the parent-of-the-year award for doing so!

52. Arrange for a back-up child-care plan when you have a sick youngster.

Parents who work full time rely on their kids attending school during the day, and having a sick child throws their work schedule and responsibilities into a spiral. Teachers cite that a lack of options for caring for a sick kid is why parents often "mask" a child's symptoms with over-the-counter cold medicine or pain medicine so the child can attend at least part of the school day. Then, when the school nurse calls, a parent may feign surprise. Keep in mind that the sick child has already informed the teacher or nurse that she was up half the night and threw up twice, so the secret is out. Some work places offer sick-child care solutions; many day care centers and community sick-child care providers often have a place where your child can rest and be taken care of until you get home.

53. Don't allow your child to play the "sick" card.

Sick is sick, and healthy is healthy. Your child needs to know that you're not going to buy a case of the "sickies" so he can get out of an assignment, sleep in, or avoid doing whatever it is he doesn't like doing. Unfortunately, most kids try (at least once) to pull off a case of the "sickies" sometime during their school years so they can stay home. School nurses comment that the same "sickies syndrome" happens during school hours, and it's hard to truly know when a child is faking. Comments like "I threw up in the toilet, and then flushed it," or, "I feel like I'm going to throw up," are able to get an intended reaction rather quickly, so parents, teachers, and the school nurse need to work together if your child has learned that pretending to be sick may mean a day with doting Mom and cartoons! Of course, none of this applies when a child is *truly* not feeling well.

54. Take age- and level-appropriate books with you wherever you go.

Travel with books in your car, take them on trips, and bring them to appointments. The books will entertain your child while waiting for the doctor, at the airport, etc., and help encourage a love of reading. If possible, find a series of books that your child likes, so when one age-appropriate book is finished, you are able to reward her with another. There are numerous elementary-age early-reader series out there, so if in doubt, ask your child's teacher.

55. Create a send-off routine each morning that will carry your child through the elementary school years.

The send-off can be as simple as, "Have a GREAT day at school and do your best!" or, "I love you forever!" Repeated every morning and even year after year, it will be something that will help reinforce a positive attitude, best effort, and of course, your love!

56. Encourage youthful spirituality in accordance with your family's beliefs.

Research has shown that youngsters who actively participate in religious worship have a lower incidence of depression than non-religious classmates. Spiritual awareness can start with the very young, and can reduce the risk of anxiety and other stress-inducing emotions. Provide your children with ample opportunities to see the "big picture" in life, and to become aware of the needs of others and their community. If your child's school uses a "moment of silence" to begin the day, encourage him to use that time to either pray or reflect on the day at hand for best effort, listening ears, and a positive attitude!

57. Ask your child's teacher how she handles a situation with her own child for good advice on an issue troubling your youngster.

Not all teachers are parents, of course, but many at your child's school are. If you are struggling with a certain issue with your child, turn the tables and ask a trusted teacher who is also a parent what she would do. Teachers are more apt to freely to express their opinion when it is not

recommending action about someone else's child.

58. Review bathroom habits with your child at every age.

Bathrooms at school are communal
property, and it's critical that your
child maintains good hygiene, such
as proper wiping, flushing the toilet
(yes, kids still forget!), and zipping
zippers and tucking in shirts. Girls
need to make sure their dresses aren't
caught in their tights and that shirt
strings aren't dunked in the toilet.
While teachers can oversee hand-
washing regiments, what happens in
a bathroom is, of course, private. But
parents can review and remind!

59. Model to your child that education is important to you today and in the future.

If you are learning something new

(such as how to operate a new camera, television remote, or appliance), tell your child how glad you are that you went to school to learn how to read the directions and learn step-by-step processes. Better yet, maybe your child can help teach you! Constant reinforcement of how much you valued your own gift of education will help your kid better appreciate hers!

60. Make sure you set aside time each day to go over your child's work so you as a parent know what is going on.

This is different than the homework time you set up for your child or when you review your child's work for the day. This is for you, as the parent, to carefully see and sometimes even learn what your child is up to at school. Once your child is through with his homework and you've checked it for understanding, look through the textbook or through notes or materials yourself. Consider it your personal homework time! Especially in the advanced elementary grades, parents are sometimes surprised to see what their child is learning. Truth be told, here's betting you don't remember every fact or how to complete every equation that your child is doing. Keep pace with your child's level of learning, and if possible, keep a step ahead.

61. Don't forget to plug in quality time over the weekend to review your child's lessons and advance needed skills.

Yes, we all need weekends to rest and chill. Saturdays are often loaded up with sports games and family activities as well. But to keep your child prepared and confident come Monday morning, try to carve out at least thirty minutes over the weekend to review any newly learned concepts and practice reading skills.

62. Proudly display your child's school accomplishments.

Whether you create a "wall of honor," attach good grades and comments to the kitchen refrigerator, or even create a child's art gallery in your home, constantly reinforce to your child that you place high value on school work. Don't just stick it in a keepsake box or haphazardly place it on the countertop; really celebrate it! For extra-special pieces, consider scanning the artwork, essay, or test grade (if you have a scanner), and sending it to grandparents or beloved family members with a note to have them call and congratulate your child. Small honors can become big and foster the love of learning and success.

63. Review your child's academic mistakes until you feel confident he has grasped the concept.

Truly understanding a lesson will make a child feel more confident the next day at school. Kids can become defensive and even secretive when they don't "get" something. In a non-threatening way, make sure to drill on those areas or talk your child through it. His self-confidence will soar as he grasps the concept.

64. Make a child's schoolwork her "job" and not just busy work or a chore.

Kids quickly can adopt a mind-set that there is a lot of "busy work" at school. Teachers will tell you that every work sheet, whether disguised as fun or as a review, leads back to the lesson being learned. Your children should know that you consider school their "full-time job," just like you have a job and related responsibilities, whether inside or outside the home.

65. If your child packs a lunch, consider buying or creating a really cool lunchbox or container that makes him feel special.

This doesn't mean you need to spend a lot of money; a paper sack can be decorated with stickers or creative artwork. The key is to make your child excited to bring lunch to school. A note tucked into the lunchbox can add an extra touch of love!

66. Model a morning and evening routine.

It's never too early to start and maintain a routine in a child's life. And the best way to start is to lead by example. Let your child see you carefully brushing your teeth and then flossing, folding pajamas and leaving them on the pillow (or whatever is your routine), and then carefully putting the hairbrush back in the drawer. Talk to your child about why you do these routines (i.e., "I put my pajamas here every morning so I always know where they are at nighttime"), and how it helps you to be better prepared to start the day.

67. Teach your child the meaning behind character traits.

Use virtue words, such as *trust*, *honesty*, and *citizenship*, in your conversations at home, and ask your child how she demonstrated a certain trait each day at school. For example, if you're talking to your child about "wisdom," you might ask what she did to demonstrate that trait at school. It sparks a conversation but will also help build an active good citizen at school.

68. **Turn off your cell phone whenever you are taking your child to school, picking him up from school, or are at the school for any reason.**

You are there for your child...so really BE there in terms of attention, please! Short of an absolute emergency, any other call can wait. Really! In addition, you yakking on your phone lets your child know he isn't your top priority. Many schools have adopted a "no cell phone" policy on school grounds and will continue to toughen the policy with time. Safety is cited as the top reason. Each year, accidents occur (usually minor, thank goodness) when kids are dropped off at school by a parent who is talking on the phone and then drives off without checking the proximity of other kids.

69. Carefully look over and talk about your child's schoolwork each day.

Your child is proud of what she did at school, and parents can deflate that when they toss their child's backpack to the side or halfheartedly look inside. Instead, take five minutes with your child for one-on-one time and ask questions, such as: "This is a great diagram of a plant. Do you know what the roots are for?" Or, "I love this math puzzle. I see you are learning fractions. Can you give me an example of a fraction?"

70. Ask your child about specific people and events.

When the time is right and you ask your child questions about his day, question him about specific people and events in a non-drilling fashion. Examples include: "Who did you sit next to on the bus home today?" "Is your teacher over her cold now?" Or, "Did you like your gym substitute teacher?" Follow up with additional cheerful or supportive comments based on how your child responds.

71. Fitness and exercise are great for kids, but not just before bedtime.

Kids who are healthy and physically fit may have better stamina and focus at school and sleep more soundly at night, as long as they don't exercise just before bedtime. Research has shown that any type of rigorous extended activity just before bedtime can keep people from going to sleep, often because they are alert or don't seem tired. Inevitably, this results in a delay in getting quality rest. The after-effect will show up the next morning when the child appears sluggish. If your child participates in extracurricular sports after school, encourage the coaches to hold practice early enough to give kids ample time to cool down and relax before hitting the books (if homework isn't yet done), having a snack or meal, and then readying for bed. Ideally, practices for younger kids should end no later than 7 p.m. If your schedule permits, exercise stretches are also a great way to begin a day!

72. Monitor your child's extracurricular participation.

Monitor your child's activities and don't allow her *or you* to go overboard in an effort to try different things for cultural or physical enrichment. Many kids have activities after school and do not even begin their homework until after dinner, meaning they are already winding down and are honest-to-goodness tired by the time they need to complete their assignments. This translates to a kid not putting forth her best effort in homework or the classroom. A good rule of thumb is no more than two extracurricular activities at any one given time. Parents of multiple children sometimes cut that back to one.

73. Help your child establish priorities at school.

Encourage your child to set academic priorities each day, such as reviewing spelling words on the bus ride, talking with a teacher about an upcoming project, or completing all projects on time in the classroom without distractions so unfinished work doesn't have to be brought home. Giving your child "chunks" of things to check on or reviewing her to-do list helps to build self-responsibility and is the first step toward creating a responsible and independent adult.

74. Empower your child to determine dedicated time for homework.

Let your child have a role in setting up a schedule for homework at home. Line up everything your child is responsible for, and then determine how much time is available and see what solutions your child can reach to make everything fall into place. Of course, you as a parent will have veto power over a plan that is not workable (and an opportunity to talk with your child why another option is needed). Discuss with your child that timing is everything when it comes to homework, and scheduling this time will be based on your child's individual temperament and schedule. Some kids like to come straight home after school and finish any projects. Others want to rest and "chill," play with friends, eat dinner, and then do homework as a way to wind down.

75. Breakfast can be the most important "brain food" of the day.

Popular cereals or powdery donuts may bring a smile to your child's face and a burst of energy when leaving for school, but that sugar rush may quickly wear off, leaving your child tired—and hungry! While it's not always practical to have a big meal of scrambled eggs and bacon every day, always encourage your child to eat a piece of fruit and something filling such as oatmeal, and drink plain milk or juice when there is a big day planned at school. For time-crunched families, consider letting your child eat breakfast at school. Many menus offer variety and over-all nutritional value, and are usually quite inexpensive—often less than you spend each day on your child's breakfast. It's another option worth considering!

76. Keep bedtime a top priority.

Every parent knows sleep is important. However, teachers report that knowing it and actually enforcing bedtime rules are two different things. Parents, you know who you are! Elementary-aged children need about ten hours of sleep, on average, and trends show that kids are increasingly staying up later, falling asleep with a television on in their room, or not getting to bed until 10 p.m. or later on school nights. Even though kids can occasionally get away with less sleep, teachers are in agreement that children without ample sleep are sluggish, overly sensitive, grumpy, and, plain and simple, not at their best the next day. Kids' bedtimes should be around 8:30 p.m., give or take thirty minutes depending on family schedules or age of the child, and without distractions that keep them from getting the very best quality sleep possible. Teachers everywhere will thank you!

77. Get to know all the staff at your child's school.

Most parents get to know their child's teacher and school principal. But to truly help your child be as successful at school as possible, take additional time and effort to become acquainted with *everyone* at school, including the nurse and librarian, music and art teachers, physical education coach, school counselor, custodian, and child nutrition and support staff. Be sure to introduce yourself to any educational assistants who may work with teachers as well. By extending a friendly hello and putting a parental face with your child's name, staff will be able to more readily learn your family's needs and better assist your child if the need arises.

78. Become acquainted with your child's friends.

A good way to stay connected with how your child is faring socially at school is to get to know his friends. Asking about friends is also a round-about way of finding out more about what your kid is doing and participating in at school. Take time to greet your child's friends when you are at school, and ask about their interests and activities. Most kids love extra attention from adults and showing off their assignments or projects. Ask a friend whether he gets to see your child often, and if so, for what class or activity. Often, you can get a more detailed response from your child's friend than from your child himself. Periodically, ask your child how their friendship is going, and whether they've done anything fun together lately.

79. Eat lunch with your child at least once a month.

Lunchtime is perhaps the most eagerly anticipated and social setting for elementary kids out of the entire school day. At many schools, having a parent come to lunch with her child is considered a very special treat. Many schools offer a separate seating area for the honored parent guests to eat with their children. Keep in mind that while your kids may clamor for you to come eat with them in elementary school, they'd be mortified if you tried to do the same in middle school. So, carve time out of your busy schedule at least once a month and have lunch with your child…while she still lets you!

80. Find out what your child is eating—really truly eating (that means chewing and swallowing!)—for lunch.

An increasing number of school districts have gone to a third-party company that allows parents to pay for their children's lunches and view purchases on a daily basis. This lets parents keep better track of their kids' diet at school. While you may not always know whether your child actually cleaned his plate or picked at the food choice, there is comfort to be found in knowing what was purchased. You might find your child is buying a dessert on a daily basis rather than once a week, as you specified, or you might take comfort in knowing your child is making sound nutritional choices. If you are worried about whether your child is truly eating the plate lunch or lunch brought from home, ask a cafeteria monitor to keep her eye on your child for a few days and report back to you. If you're packing a healthy lunch that your child is throwing away every day, it's time for Plan B.

81. Have your child exchange clothing items left at school regularly to reflect changes in season and growth.

Many parents thoughtfully tuck in a set of extra clothes, gym shoes, or a jacket when school starts, but neglect to change them out according to season or a child's growth! Remember that a child's shoe size can change dramatically over the course of a school year, and you don't want your child telling you she didn't get to participate in something or had to wear something borrowed from the office because the clothes in the locker didn't fit! Keep tabs on what your child brings to school;

there is no room in a class locker for several jackets and shoes that seem to magically accumulate over the course of a school year. Ask your child to check her locker and bring home unneeded items at least once a month.

82. Say no to tardiness.

Some parents have a "whatever" attitude about getting their children to school on time without realizing its impact. It may not seem such a big deal to get your child to school five or ten minutes late occasionally… right? Truth is, being tardy to class can be embarrassing to a child, who typically must first sign in at the office and then enter the classroom watched by twenty or so pairs of staring eyes. Inconvenience to teachers is also a factor, as the day truly begins when the school bell rings. The first few minutes of a day are when many teachers discuss daily expectations and planned activities, recite the Pledge of Allegiance, and transition kids into "school thinking." Missing that early information could affect a child's performance the rest of the day, which means a teacher must present the information again to the child who is late. Of course, being tardy due to a doctor's appointment or a related activity can't always be avoided, and teachers are always willing to help a child catch up on any missed event.

83. Limit after-school "seat time."

It's important to keep your kids active. They've had plenty of "seat time" at school; after school is the time to be on the go. Kids sitting for lessons, sitting for homework, and sitting to watch television and play video games translates into a greater potential for childhood obesity.

Don't let your kids settle into a sedentary lifestyle; find ways to keep them active. Organized sports, such as baseball or soccer, are good options, but so are family evening walks after dinner or nightly bike rides.

84. Become actively involved in your school's parent-teacher association.

Most schools have an organized parent-teacher association, and hopefully, you're already a member! If not, know this: Memberships are quite inexpensive and are renewable annually, and benefits include such activities as school carnivals, field days, field trips, and special parent education programs. Plus, the volunteer-run operation works in partnership with school staff and the principal, and together the team can help raise funding for desired supplies or special events that may not be in the district's or school's coffers. If you're not familiar with whether your school participates or promotes an association, ask your child's teacher!

85. Don't be a complainer. If you don't like something, join the committee that organizes it next time.

Don't be one of those parents who complains about everything but is involved in nothing. Remember that most activities and parties are coordinated by volunteers who are giving their time for the benefit of kids. Maybe the event isn't perfect, and you feel you can do better. Then step up next time. Meanwhile, your kid most likely won't notice the small details about what is wrong—only that he is having fun!

86. Ask your child with a case of "I can'ts" to tell you about a time when she could.

Some kids can sail through almost any new project or concept. Others, however, are tentative and so fearful of failure that they don't even attempt to try. Some children (and adults, too) feel it is safer to say, "I can't," than to try and possibly not succeed. An unwillingness to try something new can put a quick halt to a child's learning of a new subject or concept. Instead of pushing your child to "just try," start by talking about something she was previously afraid to try, but eventually worked up her courage and now can do quite well! Whether it's learning to swim, attempting a cartwheel, or even boarding a school bus, talk about how your child has already overcome other things in her life. It might be helpful for you to reveal some of your former "I can't" secrets that you've now worked through (such as learning a new computer system at work). Realizing that she isn't alone in her reluctance to try something new or different sometimes helps a child think through what is needed to tackle the new assignment. Finally, be sure to offer lots of praise and hugs because attempting something new is a huge accomplishment in its own right!

87. Remember that your child needs unconditional love.

Unconditional love means exactly that, and your child should never be made to feel that grades, a performance in a school play, or the science fair influences how much you love him. Parents need to be sure that their expressions of love match their words; kids tend to look first at expressions for support and reassurance.

So don't be afraid to hug your child and smile even when on the inside you don't think there is much to smile about! Your support is what your child craves most for overall school success.

88. Praise a child's effort, not the outcome, even if the outcome is less than ideal.

Emphasize to your child that in life it's not how you fail, but how you get back up again after a stumble. It's a lesson your child can take with her for the rest of her life!

89. Ask your child's teacher for a copy of the classroom's rules.

Most teachers adopt a set of basic classroom rules, many of which are set by the kids themselves at the start of every school year. Those rules are posted throughout the year and referenced frequently in terms of behavior, work effort, and how to treat one another. Ask your child's teacher for a copy so you can also review them with your child at home throughout the year. If your child behaves in a way at home that isn't in keeping with expectations at school, you can remind your kid why it would not be acceptable at class as another reinforcement measure.

90. Teach your child about diversity and tolerance.

If you haven't already done so, have a talk with your child about diversity and tolerance. Kids should be taught to accept, if not embrace, different skin tones, races, religious differences, or physical differences. Take advantage of holidays as an opportunity to either teach or augment what your child is learning in school by bringing up differences. A great opportunity for instilling tolerance and enthusiasm about differences is around the winter holiday season and all the religious and cultural celebrations. In addition, you can talk to your child about how these holidays are celebrated differently around the world. Repeat similar "learning moments" throughout the year.

91. Give your child a schedule rundown before he leaves home each day to avoid unanticipated surprises.

Remind your child that church choir practice will be at 7 p.m. or that dance practice begins right after school as a way to help him sort and plan out his day. Kids like to know what's next in their lives, and keeping them posted helps them feel more in control.

92. If your kid leaves something important at home that she needs at school, remind her

you love her, but don't rescue her unless she's a very young child and you truly have the time.

Yes, it's stressful for you to hear that the homework project your child toiled over (and you helped review) was left on the kitchen table and will now be counted late. It's stressful news for your child too, but don't let the paper ruin her whole day. Still tell her you love her and send her into school with a hug, even though you both know the assignment won't get turned in. The key is to not have a child glum throughout the day. After all, there is always tomorrow (and then a review of where finished homework assignments should go!).

93. **Take advantage of as many school offerings as possible. Remember that they are all**

tied into some component of education.

Whether it's math club, writing club, the spelling bee, choir, or other activities, the more school-related activities your children can participate in within reason, the happier and more successful they'll probably be. Be careful about over-scheduling your child, however. You want to leave plenty of time in the day for simple outdoor fun, family time, rest and relaxation, and homework!

94. **If your child has not had a good morning before school, mention a silly joke or funny family event to lighten the send-off.**

Whatever "happy time" send-off works best for your child, be sure to drop him off to school with a smile. Consider getting a kid-friendly joke book that you use as your secret weapon before going to school. Plus, your kid will then have a fresh joke to tell to his friends!

95. Add music to your family's daily routine.

Numerous studies have shown the academic and emotional benefit of music in a child's life. Find ways to include music in your home, whether by playing upbeat songs and singing together on the way to school, playing soothing music at bedtime, or even having classical music playing in the background during dinner each evening. Encourage your child to really listen to the melodies, guess which instruments are making particular sounds, and encourage originality in singing or humming! If your child has a music program at school, be sure to get to know the music teacher and keep track of what your child is learning to reinforce the musical knowledge at home.

96. If it's a test day, make sure your child knows how much you believe in her.

Important test days need extra preparation by parents, so kids can do their best without worrying about their clothes, breakfast, lunch, or getting to school on time. An extra-big smile should be on your face from wake-up until send-off, and the last thing your child should hear from you before entering school is that you believe in her and that all you expect is that she gives her best effort.

97. Incorporate computer time at home for educational purposes, if possible.

Without a doubt, computers in the classroom are becoming a reality everywhere, and as early as preschool, kids are learning keyboarding and mousing skills. Some kids find that learning to read is easier with computer prompts; others like to write and solve math problems. Most likely, your child's school has a computer lab; but regardless of whether it does or not, you should teach your child to use a computer at home for educational purposes. There are countless educational websites that can help answer questions about the world, and kids love the way a computer can help them find an answer they can read about and see at the same time. Don't let your kid have free use of the computer, however, without parental locks and supervision in place. Computer time should always be in a controlled setting.

98. Make sure you follow all school-related parent requirements.

If the teacher asks that parents sign a daily planner that acknowledges homework, conduct, etc., don't forget! Nothing stresses a child out more. In fact, for many kids, opening the planner to find an empty space where your signature should be can put a damper on the child's entire day. Think of parent requirements as *your* homework and responsibility.

99. Make a game of leaving Post-It notes in silly places.

Your child will delight in finding notes from you (or even the family dog, for example) lovingly tucked in different places. A note can be as simple as a smiley face tucked in his gym shoes, pencil bag, lunch box, planner, snack bag, or even in the arm of a jacket. Your child may not tell you how much he appreciates it, but it's guaranteed to bring a smile to his face and warm his heart.

100. Ask your child about what bothers her.

If your kid seems moody or withdrawn, see if you can draw out the problem by asking questions about whether the class started a new unit of study, if anyone bothered her, or if she and her best friend bickered again at recess. Since people in general like to complain about things that aren't quite right, it might be possible to find the root of the problem and then take steps to help make tomorrow's school day brighter.

101. Plan report-card celebration days, even if grades are lower than you'd like them to be.

Don't fall in the parent trap of celebrating only As and creating the impression that anything lower is unacceptable. You're setting your child up for failure with that attitude. While you want your child to get high grades, the truth is that not all kids are straight-A students. And in case you haven't noticed, school is a lot harder than it was when most of us were kids, and most kids of today are getting more homework. In addition, teachers are increasingly being tasked to grade assignments in all subject areas, whereas previously subjects such as art, music, and physical education didn't receive a letter grade at the elementary level. If you know your child tried his hardest, celebrate his accomplishments come report-card time. Keep in mind the big picture: Yes, your child got a B in math, but he was able to master the multiplication tables after a lot of effort. On a separate occasion, talk with your child about how he felt about his grades, and identify areas you can help him with for the next grading period. Kids should feel excited about showing parents their report cards, and if you observe your child trying to hide them or become withdrawn or even afraid to show his results, you might re-examine your approach to grades.

102. Start a Sunday-night back-to-school ritual that is fun for your child.

Whether it's planning a silly Sunday, a favorite family dinner-and-movie night, or a bubble fun in the bathtub, create an event that is eagerly anticipated and only occurs on Sunday night. Don't tie it into going to school; just make it a fun way to welcome in each week. If your child is happy on Sunday, the start of the work and school week will potentially be a much happier time for everyone!

103. Know that the "Monday morning blues" can affect kids, too.

To ward off any Monday-morning blues, set your alarm early on Monday mornings to give yourself a few extra minutes to help your child eat a well-balanced breakfast, get dressed and ready on time, and have a few remaining minutes to receive a cheery send-off (and not a "push-off"). Consider starting a Friday countdown that begins on each Monday, or start a countdown to another activity that your child looks forward to each week.

104. While reading with your child, pause occasionally to verbalize your personal thoughts.

Part of building critical thinking and deductive reasoning skills and developing a deeper understanding of content is being able to predict what will happen next, muse over actions and events, and even analyze characters. Parents can help elementary-age kids build skills by modeling these thoughts out loud and encouraging discussion. You can say things like, "I think Emily behaved rather badly in the story. I could tell in the first chapter that she likes to get other kids in trouble. What do you think? How do you think I knew that she might be a troublemaker?"

105. Make your refrigerator your family's first source for all school-related news.

Maybe it creates a little clutter, but truthfully there is NO better place to post upcoming school activities, spelling words, projects, etc., than on the appliance that is looked at and opened multiple times a day. Post teacher notes, due dates, the school calendar, and schedules at eye level, and develop a routine where it is the first place you look when mulling over meal planning or getting a glass of milk.

106. You're really not bothering the teacher with your questions.

Parents often feel they are bothering or bogging down a teacher with questions, comments, or concerns. But teachers readily agree that they'd love to get MORE questions from parents throughout the school year and not just when report cards are in. It's okay to call or email a teacher to clarify a due date or confirm a project's scope. Really! By the same token, remember your desire for immediate information may not work with a teacher's schedule. Except for a conference period, which is filled with many job-related responsibilities, a teacher may need to answer you before or after classes each day and keep the focus on classroom needs during school hours.

107. Avoid embarrassing your child about homework concepts— even if you've gone over them dozens of times.

Kids learn at different paces, and while it may be frustrating if your child is not "getting" something, keep in mind the same thing was probably said or thought about *you* during *your* early school years, as well. Almost every parent at some time has said something like, "How could you have missed that on the test? We spent all week, every night, for an hour going over this. You had it down. What happened?" Instead, bite your tongue and offer reassurance with a comment like this: "I see we need to work on this some more. Don't worry. You'll get it. Maybe tonight we can review it outside, if the weather holds."

108. Your child needs to know that sometimes it's okay to fail.

Many successes are built out of failures. If your child is suffering from low self-esteem or a sagging confidence level about some low grades or other school performance (such as not getting picked for a part in the school play), have a heart-to-heart talk about failure. Kids need to know that not succeeding at something doesn't make them a failure. They may have "failed" a test or "failed" to get a part, but that doesn't mean they can't do something to turn that lack of success into something they are proud of. Teachers are all too willing to work with kids to bring up grades or provide additional assistance, and your child can ask to operate the stage curtain or do something special to contribute to the school play that doesn't involve a part onstage. It's not just okay to talk about your own shortcomings as a parent when you were in school—it's healthy! Chances are, you still remember some failures and how you overcame them, so share them with your child. Kids should not be told that if they work hard they'll always get what they want, because that's not reality. Kids who work hard *will* be more successful overall!

109. Don't let a child see you become frustrated with anything related to school.

It's sometimes easy to become frustrated or discouraged if a project you helped oversee comes back with a mediocre grade, and you thought it deserved an A! Of course you did— you're the parent! Don't give in to outbursts or negative comments or in any way show your emotions to your child. Instead, try to find out what details or information were lacking so your child can be better prepared next time. Chances are, the teacher will include a critique or assessment to help kids and their parents better understand the grade. If you still feel frustrated after reading any teacher notes, schedule a one-on-one conference with the teacher. Be sure to offer praise to your child for a job completed, and let her know that you're proud it was turned in on time and with lots of effort. There's always that next assignment ahead!

110. Your child's grade on a test isn't a direct reflection of your parenting.

It's easy to fall into the trap of thinking that you did something wrong if your child didn't perform well on a test. Keep in mind, however, that some kids simply don't take tests well due to anxiety or not feeling well. Test-taking is a learned skill that requires practice and extra effort for many children. If you reviewed material with your child until you felt comfortable he knew the subject, and he still didn't get a good score, realize that the teacher most likely knows which students grasped the information already, and that your child simply needs more test prep in the future!

111. Make an attempt to understand why your child is being tested using various state assessments, benchmarks, and national comparisons before passing judgment.

Many parents are critical of the testing a young child must complete each year, yet in the next breath they may demand to know how their child is doing compared with peers or how the school is doing compared with other schools. Benchmarks help educators see where a child's strengths and weaknesses may be in a variety of subjects so teaching can be targeted to those areas. Ask your teacher for a conference to have her explain the various tests for your child's age and grade, and then to review your child's results with you. You have the right to view your child's educational records and testing results, and upon closer analysis, you may find areas that you can enhance at home in partnership with the school!

112. Make sure your child can safely carry around her backpack once it's loaded with her homework.

Picking out a trendy backpack with the latest action hero or ultra cool style is one thing. But backpacks loaded with textbooks, planners, lunches, and anything else a child may tote can be a health or safety hazard if it's too heavy. Improperly used backpacks can cause severe neck, back, and shoulder pain. Check with your child occasionally to see if her backpack is causing any discomfort. If so, either consider buying a new backpack in a different style or check with the teacher to see if any of the books can be kept at home for reference instead of being brought back and forth each day.

113. Don't teach your child short-cuts for getting an answer.

In elementary school, most teachers emphasize that kids must show their work and follow a step-by-step process. The reasoning is not to create extra work; rather, showing work helps demonstrate that a child understands all the steps needed to reach the right solution. Well-meaning parents who show kids tricks or techniques to reach the right answer may actually cause their child's work to be marked wrong for not showing all the steps. Remember that shortcuts can be used in later school years, but for now, support what your child's teacher is trying to instill.

114. Teach your child how to tie his shoes.

This may seem like a "duh" hint for some, but many kids in first, second, and even third grade don't know how to tie their shoes properly (popular shoe styles without laces could be the culprit). If laces aren't tied properly, they're always coming undone—at the risk of a child getting hurt by tripping over them. Practice tying laces with your child until shoes can consistently be laced tightly. Until then, have your child wear

Velcro or pull-on shoes at school for safety's sake.

115. Make sure your child understands that it is his job—not his teacher's—to pick up his trash, push in his chair, and clear his desk.

Picking up classrooms each day is a frustrating and time-consuming activity for teachers. While custodial help may be available at the school, kids should be taught to throw away their trash, push in their chairs, put their supplies away neatly, hang their jackets in the lockers, and keep P.E. shoes tucked away. These are simple things for kids to do, but teachers lament that due to lack of reinforcement at home, some kids have to be told the same thing day after day and week after week, all year long. Even notes home requesting help don't always work. Talk to your child about common school etiquette, and tell him you will ask the teacher to let you know if he does not keep up his personal space in the classroom to the level desired by the teacher. Inform the teacher that you want to know, and then apply any consequences if needed. (Note: One brave teacher requires any child who has to be reminded more than twice in a six-week reporting period to perform custodial duties for the entire classroom for a week. She says that it works every time!)

116. Show your child how to relax!

We're not talking spa treatments or deep-tissue massages, but help teach your kid how to develop her very own self-calming and relaxing techniques. Next time your child appears stressed, encourage her to lay down flat, close her eyes, take deep, cleansing breaths, and imagine "happy thoughts." Soft music is another suggestion, as music therapy has been shown to reduce anxiety in different kinds of situations. Encourage your child to come up with her own unique way of relaxing and to invite you to join her (or not). Have your child develop a "quick-fix" relaxation technique for the classroom, where it isn't feasible to lie down and turn on music. One idea is to roll shoulders backward and then forward, and then roll the neck clockwise and counter clockwise while breathing deeply and slowly. Relaxation skills can carry your child through the years ahead in the classroom, and after that, into the working world!

117. Seek out books that supplement what your child is learning at school.

If your child is learning about the Civil War, for example, look for age-appropriate books (and there are many) about the time period that your child can read with you. There are countless exciting science books that closely track what elementary students are learning (the study of weather is always a favorite topic, for example). If possible, find nearby historical reminders of past occurrences and plan a visit, or make a virtual visit on the Internet. A trip to historic buildings, birthplaces of your country's leaders, or other landmarks can forever impress on a young mind that what they are learning about *really did* happen.

118. Let things go a little.

Well-meaning parents sometimes put too much pressure on their kids, and rather than stimulating a child's thirst for knowledge, they actually end up causing emotional damage. Sometimes this means letting go of your own parental neediness and not pressuring your child to win the spelling bee because you never did.

119. Avoid dehydration. Have your child pack a water bottle for school every day.

Most schools allow kids to bring water bottles to class. Having water bottles readily available helps eliminate the disruption of getting up for a sip of water throughout the day. It's best to choose a water bottle with a sports top (versus the kind that screws off and is left open for consumption) to minimize spills and ruined assignments.

120. Don't ever "enable" your child to not complete a project or other work.

Teachers indicate that parents are often the culprit behind a child's failure to complete a project or work, because perhaps they haven't bought a required poster board or checked out a book their child needs for the project. When the deadline arrives and the work isn't done, parents then want their child to give an excuse or ask for an extension. Usually, that "second chance" doesn't come automatically, but with a learning moment attached. Some teachers may require a child and her parent to conference with them directly to explain responsibilities and review communications that were sent out with the requirements and the established deadline. Even if an extension is granted, or a late grade (with points taken off) is allowed, assignments should be taken seriously and turned in, with best effort, on time. This sets a good example for upcoming years of homework.

121. Take a class photo and label all the kids' names on it for display in your child's room.

Ask your child's teacher to let you take a group photo of the class (and give her a copy to display in the classroom). Put a child's name to each face by labeling it either on the computer or on a sheet of paper attached to a printed photo, and then display it in your child's room throughout the current school year. This not only helps your child remember names but also keeps him familiar with classmates and his "school family" throughout the year!

122. Show your child how to create one-of-a-kind book covers for textbooks.

Sure, you can buy one of those colorful, stretchy book covers from a big box store. Or you can show your child how to make a one-of-a-kind cover from a decorated paper bag, wrapping paper, or any other type of "wrapping." Since textbooks are used for several years, most schools require that textbooks be covered to help protect them against wear and tear. Let your child show her style, love of space, or a favorite color or interest that will bring a smile when the book is used! Some creative kids even change out their textbook covers for the holidays, using wrapping paper showcasing Halloween, Christmas, Valentine's Day, or other noteworthy days. Clever!

123. Encourage spontaneous free play.

Every minute of your child's life shouldn't be structured. Kids need to be kids and get the opportunity to create their own games, interests, and even rules and routines. Be sure you're providing your child with daily chunks of time to just play…without relating it to homework, mealtime, or any parental motivation. The best part? Free play *is* a form of learning. Playing outdoors, for example, is one way to let your child experience nature first-hand and touch, feel, see, and experience the wind, dirt, leaves, etc., without reading about it in books or seeing it on television.

124. Don't make your child the school messenger.

In the event of a circumstance beyond your child's control, such as a family emergency, write a note in a sealed envelope that your child can give to the teacher, call the teacher directly, or send an email if you know the teacher checks the account regularly. Or call the front office and ask for a message to be relayed. Do not ask your child to relay this information. A child may not always have all the information or facts to correctly relate a circumstance, or may become confused and provide incorrect information. Remember that in the event of a family emergency or crisis, teachers are typically more than willing to do whatever is necessary to help your child, including allowing extra time to turn in work.

125. Check in with the teacher if you don't think your child is bringing home assignments and notes.

If you find your child's "to-go-home" folder empty more often than not, be sure to check with the child's teacher to make sure that all information is coming home that should. Sometimes, kids forget to put handouts in their folders; occasionally, kids think if it doesn't go home, they don't have to do it. Teachers will increasingly task kids to be responsible for putting their folders, planners, and any required textbooks or materials in their backpacks each day, but elementary-age kids will typically require adult oversight in making sure everything gets done and returned properly!

126. Know when report cards are distributed.

Most districts mark grading periods on publicly-distributed school calendars. If yours does not, make sure you know when each period ends and report cards should be coming. Find out if your child's school also issues progress reports to keep even a clearer handle on how your kid is performing in the classroom.

127. Maintain proper portion control when packing your child's lunch.

Make your child a favorite sandwich,

throw in a bag of chips and an individual package of cookies along with a drink, and you're good to go for lunch. Right? Not so fast, say child nutritionists. Read nutrition labels and portion sizes carefully, and you'll often find that an individual pack includes six cookies, and a bag of chips is actually two servings. Given the choice between a sandwich and lots of cookies and chips, which items do you think most kids will eat first? That leaves them with a stomach full of junk food that's high in sugars and fats, putting the afternoon on high alert for disruption or lack of focus. Instead of tossing pre-packaged goodies into your child's lunchbox, break open the pre-packaging to give your child a realistic serving size of a sweet treat.

128. Don't give your child everything she asks for.

This sounds more like parenting advice than school success, but giving your child everything she wants affects how she interacts with peers at school. An elementary-age student who frequently brags about getting the latest gaming console, all the hot new games, an iPod, or even a cell phone—especially when the gifts come frequently and are expensive—is not likely to make many friends. After all, nobody likes a braggart, especially a kid who always has more than anyone else. When your child does get a pricey present, encourage her to remain low-key about it, and use the opportunity to talk about boasting and how it makes others feel. Kids who get everything they want also tend to be more demanding and tend to develop an entitlement attitude, which affects their social development and interaction with adults.

129. Don't overreact to information your child tells you.

Of course you want to protect your child and for everyone to be nice, but don't be a mama (or papa) bull on the charge when your child tells you "so-and-so was mean to me today." Often, parents just hear the outcome of the story and not necessarily the events that led up to the action, which may even be exaggerated or distorted in the first place. Instead, make sure your child knows that the teacher is always there if needed, and encourage your child and his friend to talk things through. Who knows? Tomorrow, they may be best buddies!

130. Avoid having your child bring money to school, if possible.

There are many other ways to pay

for school trips, lunch funds, or other extras than by having your child bring cash to school. That's a lot of responsibility for a young child, and there's always the possibility that she will lose the money or even have it taken away by others. Rather than risk something happening to it, take money to the school's front office, use online payments for lunch funds (if available), or at the very least, have your child bring in a check with its purpose marked on it and the "to" section filled out. At the same time, use these opportunities to start teaching your child about the value of money. Your child should learn how much lunch costs every day, what the price is of any "extras" in the serving line, and even how much it costs to go on a field trip or buy a pencil.

131. Teach your child to tell time.

Have you ever noticed how many

clocks there are in a school? That's so teachers can keep up with "school time" for classes, labs, lunch, library visits, and of course, ever-important recess! Your child will most likely want to keep up, too, so teach him how to tell time at the youngest age possible. Even better, buy your child a kid-friendly watch to develop a life-long good habit of keeping track of time. You might also consider buying an alarm clock for your child's room and encouraging him to wake himself up and begin getting ready when the alarm goes off in the morning. This is yet another step toward growing up and eventual independence. Kids can start with digital clocks but need to learn how to read a traditional clock as well.

132. Make your child a "star student."

Create a "star wall" in your home of "star" qualities achieved during the school year. These qualities can be mastery of a certain reading level, becoming the best jump-roper in the class, passing the math facts quiz, or getting an A on a history presentation. A brief summary written on a paper star does the trick and is yet another way to show your child how much you support her learning!

133. Attend every school function you can with your child.

Don't let your kid get left out of school carnivals, Valentine dances, holiday shops, and any other activity your school offers because of your schedule or lack of desire. Make it a priority to attend as many school-related activities as possible; by middle school, your child would rather you stayed home!

134. Pack a couple of napkins in your child's lunch.

Lunchroom monitors say that napkins from home seem to be in short supply, and while there are napkins available in the lunch line, kids who bring their lunches go straight to their tables. At many schools, kids are not able to get up and move freely around the cafeteria to get napkins and other things that weren't in lunch boxes. Since few younger kids are able to eat a meal without getting an embarrassing case of the dribbles or spills, a festive napkin (to keep up with holidays or in a bright color) not only serves to keep your child's face and hands clean and hopefully protect clothes, but it'll brighten his lunch day as well!

135. Let your child know that it is okay not to like someone—but that it's not okay to show it.

Kids can sometimes be cruel, often without even meaning to. There may be kids who don't like your child (although for the life of you, you can't figure out why), and others whom your child dislikes as well. Impress on your child that it is okay to like some people as friends while not liking others. But also communicate that it is NOT okay to act out or in any way show a feeling of dislike. Explain that in school, sports, enrichment activities, and even the adult world of work, there will always be people you like and those you don't. Those feelings are to be kept on the inside, and a person should always be courteous and respectful on the outside. Talk to your child about ways to act around others without hurting feelings or getting angry.

136. Show your child that math is part of everyday life.

Let your child figure out the right amount of money to give a cashier at a fast-food window and count the change that is given back. Explain why and how you balance your checkbook. Math is in everything we do—let it become part of your child's life. Always look for math-related questions to ask your child: "How many subjects do you have each day in school? Of those, how many of those have reading time, which leaves how many?" Or, "How many kids are in your class? How many are boys? So, what can we do to figure out how many girls there are?" Once you begin thinking of math in the real world, you can use life experiences to help your child become a stronger mathematical thinker!

137. Encourage your child's participation in school charity drives.

It's one thing for your family to be a charitable giver; it's another for your child to personally help with efforts and make an individual contribution. Look over the array of charitable activities and events taking place at your child's school, such as coat drives, tutoring of younger students, canned food drives to help the hungry, family "adoptions" for the holidays (to help with gifts and essentials), visits to senior citizens, etc., and let your child pick something he's interested in participating in.

138. Lead an event or activity at school each year on behalf of your child.

Kids love to see their parents involved with their school, and what better way to help make a difference and make your own child proud of you than to take on a special duty or event each year at school. Schools clamor for volunteer hands to help with special activities, to raise money for needed items, to book field trips, or to head up teacher appreciation week. Whatever it is, let your child see you doing something on behalf of the school that goes beyond her individual classroom. You'll be showing her you care about the school's well-being as a whole, and she will delight in being able to help out (even if it's just carrying in a report to the campus principal).

139. Visit the school library with your child.

Even a school library can be intimidating for a young child. There are so many books on a wide variety of topics, and knowing where to look and what even to "do" in a library may make some youngsters uncomfortable. While librarians and assistants certainly do their part in introducing children to the concept of a library, you can provide one-on-one time with your child and personally answer any questions. Help your child find sections of the library with books of interest that are age appropriate and at the proper reading level, and encourage him to check out a book. Your child should grow to eagerly await library visits and feel ever-so-grown-up when picking out a book to read and return for another one. You can further instill the concept that visiting the library is a very special occasion by presenting your child with a special bookmark, or making one together.

140. Make sure your child knows the national and state pledges

and how to place the correct hand over her heart.

Parents may consider it ever-so-cute when a young child attempts the pledge but inserts words that are wrong or are run together. But learning the correct words will be important as a child goes through school. Many schools start the day by having children recite the U.S. Pledge of Allegiance followed by the state's pledge. Have your child recite the pledges to you and then clarify the correct words without being critical. Also, help your child understand why students recite the pledge(s) each day and why it is important to pay attention and be respectful.

141. Give your child coping tips for interacting with kids at school.

For most kids, school is where they make the most friends. Unless your family moves to a new school district, your child will most likely interact with the same group of friends through elementary and into secondary school. Consider yourself a character expert on tips and techniques to make friends, keep friends, and interact with peers with other interests in their grade. Encourage ongoing talks with your child on how to best handle situations as they arise, such as wanting to be someone's best friend (which makes another kid jealous), hating their assigned seat in the lunchroom, or figuring out who to play with on the playground when different groups each want to play, which can lead to hurt feelings.

142. If your child is having a rough day or week, let him bring a small comfort item to school (as long as it's not against school rules).

Most schools do not allow children to bring large toys or personal items to the classroom, but small objects that can be kept tucked away in a backpack and out of view are typically okay. Let your child bring a favorite small stuffed animal, a hand-size ball, or some other keepsake to provide comfort during the day. If you feel it's necessary, talk with your child's teacher about it to get an okay first. You could also tuck in a wallet-size family photo or small photos of the family pets to help a child feel better at school.

143. Have your child leave the cell phone and other pricey gadgets at home.

Whether or not you feel your elementary-age child needs a cell phone or an iPod is a personal family decision. But those pricey gadgets should remain at home to prevent them from being lost or stolen, to keep your child from pulling them out to show them off, or even to make calls to you or another loved one during the school day! Educators bemoan that cell phone usage and texting causes all sorts of undue distractions at the secondary level, and there is really no place for such devices at elementary schools. If you do want your child to carry a cell phone for emergencies or for before- or after-school time, check with the school to see if it is even allowed. If so, set very strict requirements for its usage.

Above all, be sure the phone's ringer is turned to silent!

144. Be aware of any students with food allergies in your child's class, and spread the word if your child has allergies.

If you're providing snacks for the class to celebrate a special holiday or other event, be sure to ask first if any child has a food allergy to avoid any health concerns. If your child has an allergy—especially a potentially dangerous one like an allergy to peanuts or eggs—you may want to be the food/snack coordinator for the year to avoid any food on the child's "no-no" list from being served. Read labels carefully to double-check for any "hidden" ingredients. Many schools require that any food items being brought into a classroom for sharing must be made commercially (not from private kitchens) with a comprehensive list of ingredients clearly marked on the packaging. While most everyone agrees that there's nothing quite as good as homemade treats, these requirements are in place because health conditions in private homes cannot be ensured, and there is no way to validate with absolute certainty the ingredients used in a particular recipe.

145. Give your child a subscription to a kid-focused magazine.

Whether it's a magazine like *National Geographic Kids*, *Highlights*, or *American Girl*, having a magazine in your child's name will encourage a stronger love for reading on topics of interest. Plus, getting something in the mail is always exciting. Look for a magazine that has articles and photographs your child will look forward to reading. After reading, take time to discuss the content. You may find you learn a few things yourself! When your child is through with the magazine, donate it to the classroom for other kids to enjoy as well and to add to the teacher's personal resource library.

146. Praise your child's maturity and preparedness for the next grade.

Encourage your child's learning progress by promoting preparedness for the next grade and discussing subjects and topics he'll be learning there. Kids sometimes fear leaving their current grade and the sense of comfort that comes with it, so introducing your child to the next year's teachers at school social events, walking down the hallways of older grades, and even talking about exciting field trips the older students attend will help your youngster be enthusiastic about advancing a grade next year.

147. Encourage your child to write thank-you notes to helpful school personnel as situations warrant.

Thanking people who have had a positive influence on your life is always appreciated, and a heartfelt and handwritten note from a child can be more meaningful than a gift. A thank-you note doesn't need to be for the end of school only. Help your child to get into the practice of thanking a music teacher for the school musical; the P.E. coach for introducing cup stacking as an activity; and the principal for hosting a school-wide field day. Plus, writing a note helps a child practice the essential skills of critical thinking, reading, and creative writing.

148. Walk the hallways of your child's school often to see the new displays and units of study.

Want to know what's going on at your child's school? After checking in at the front office, of course, walk around the school to view the array of artwork, special announcements, notices of upcoming productions, and even lists of honor-roll and perfect-attendance honorees. A stroll through the school's halls quickly reveals current units of study as well the emerging skills of student scholars. It's a great way for parents to stay connected with school happenings.

149. Understand that your child may be more emotional at the end of the day.

Kids often save up their feelings for their parents, afraid to show their true emotions or any distress at school. Because your child trusts you, she will often tell you about the day's "recess disaster," even when her teacher reports that she had a great day at school. Kids surge with feelings and may let their emotions out by picking on a sibling, being snappish, or even sulking. The good news is that a home-cooked meal, love, and rest will help make a hard day a thing of the past.

150. Keep constant check of your child's "brat potential."

We all want to think of our offspring as lil' darlings, but truth is that some kids can exhibit brat-like behavior at school. As kids get more comfortable with a school environment surrounded by friends, some not-so-nice traits may begin to emerge. Whether it's excluding certain classmates from games at recess, not letting someone sit next to them on the bus, or hiding a classmate's pencil when he's not looking, keep constant tabs on your child's behavior to make sure that your princess isn't turning into a diva, or your prince into a schoolyard snob. Ask your child's teacher to let you know of any unacceptable behaviors, and nip them in the bud immediately to diminish the likelihood of those brat-like traits becoming part of your child's personality.

151. Make sure your child knows his left from his right.

When the teacher says "line up to my left," save your child the embarrassment of not knowing which side is correct. Younger kids may need frequent reminders of left from right, both from their own perspective (i.e., "That is my left arm") to pointing out the left side of the stage or right side of the stairs. Kids should also know whether they write or play left-handed or right-handed, and they should be willing to speak to teachers and coaches if they need help or special equipment.

About the Author

Robin McClure is a professional writer as well as a wife and busy mom of two elementary-age children and one teenager. She has written the About.com Guide to Child Care since 2004 and has worked in the fields of public and continuing education for fourteen years. She has written two books for the Playskool series published by Sourcebooks, Inc.: *The Playskool Guide to Baby Play* (2007) and *The Playskool Toddler's Busy Play Book* (2007). In addition, she has written the companion book to *151 Ways to Help Your Child Have a Great Day at School*, which is entitled *151 Ways to Start the School Year Off Right*.